I Believe & I Declare

OGOCHUKWU VERA NNAKWE
Illustrated by Kimberly Merritt

Negative emotions are toxic and can wreak havoc on a child's physical and emotional health. I Believe and I Declare was written to inspire and teach children of all ages the power of positive thinking. As the little ones in your life proclaim the powerful truths written in this book, they will develop a healthy self-esteem, boosting their confidence and helping them overcome bullying, peer pressure, poor body image, or any other challenge they may be facing.

Young readers will enjoy the colorful illustrations that support the important message of the book. The biblically sound text is coupled with thought provoking pictures.

I believe:

God has a purpose in my life.
He created me in His own image.
He has shaped me into what I am today.
He will continue to mold me into what
He wants me to be tomorrow.

*"For I know the plans I have for you," declares the Lord,
"plans to prosper you and not to harm you, plans to give you hope and a future."*
— Jeremiah 29:11

I believe:

God's promises to me are true and they will come to pass.
God's will is eternal and whatever He has done in my life will last forever.
God knew me before I was born.
God wants what's best for me.

*"Before I formed you in the womb I knew you,
before you were born I set you apart."*

—Jeremiah 1:5

I believe:

God loves to reveal Himself to me.

God will bless whatever my hands touch.

God will bless my coming and going.

God blesses me so I can be a blessing to others.

All these blessings will come on you and accompany you if you obey the Lord your God:

You will be blessed in the city and blessed in the country.

The fruit of your womb will be blessed, and the crops of your land and the young of your livestock—the calves of your herds and the lambs of your flocks. Your basket and your kneading trough will be blessed.

You will be blessed when you come in and blessed when you go out. The Lord will grant that the enemies who rise up against you will be defeated before you. They will come at you from one direction but flee from you in seven.

The Lord will send a blessing on your barns and on everything you put your hand to. The Lord your God will bless you in the land he is giving you.

The Lord will establish you as his holy people, as he promised you on oath, if you keep the commands of the Lord your God and walk in obedience to him. Then all the peoples on earth will see that you are called by the name of the Lord, and they will fear you. The Lord will grant you abundant prosperity—in the fruit of your womb, the young of your livestock and the crops of your ground—in the land he swore to your ancestors to give you. The Lord will open the heavens, the storehouse of his bounty, to send rain on your land in season and to bless all the work of your hands. You will lend to many nations but will borrow from none. The Lord will make you the head, not the tail. If you pay attention to the commands of the Lord your God that I give you this day and carefully follow them, you will always be at the top, never at the bottom.

— Deuteronomy 28:2-13

I believe:

God is transforming me right now.

God is making me the best version of myself that I could ever be.

God is filling me more and more with His Holy Spirit.

God is restoring, renewing, reviving, and rekindling His joy in me every day.

"The joy of the Lord is your strength."

—Nehemiah 8:10

I can do all this through him who gives me strength.

— Philippians 4:13

I believe:

I am enough in God because God is enough in me.

I will make it.

I will not be defeated.

I can trust God to take me to places that I never imagined.

I believe:

God is greater in me than whatever problem I may face.

God works all things together for my good because I love Him.

God can turn stumbling blocks into stepping-stones.

God will give me strength for every challenge I face. I will keep trying. I will keep fighting. I will never give up. He will cause me to triumph in complete victory.

And we know that in all things God works for the good of those who love him, who have been called according to his purpose.
— Romans 8:28

I believe:

God loves me and has my name written
on the palm of His hands.

God's thoughts toward me are precious.

God will never leave me or forsake me.

God will fight for me.

"Be strong and
courageous. Do not
be afraid or terrified
because of them, for
the LORD your God
goes with you; he will
never leave you nor
forsake you."

— Deuteronomy 31:6

Trust in the Lord with all your heart and lean not on your own understanding; in all your ways submit to him, and he will make your paths straight.

— Proverbs 3:5-6

I believe:

I can trust God and He will direct my path.

God will lead me to the right place at the right time.

God is trustworthy and those who trust Him fully find Him wholly true.

God will give me Kingdom connections for His divine purposes.

I believe:

God will turn every test into a testimony.

God will help me look at my abilities
not my disabilities.

God is bigger than any mountain
I am facing.

God will turn every mess
in to a message.

And my God will meet all your needs
according to the riches of his
glory in Christ Jesus.
— Philippians 4:19

I believe:

I am made in God's image to achieve greatness for His honor and glory.

No weapon formed against me can prosper.

Each day is a gift and I will celebrate the present moment.

My past cannot dictate my future.

No weapon that is formed against thee shall prosper.

— Isaiah 54:17 KJV

I believe:

My body is a temple of the Holy Spirit.
God is my great Physician.
My health is in God's hands.
God will give me divine health.

There shall no evil befall thee,
neither shall any plague come nigh thy dwelling.
— Psalm 91:10 KJV

Therefore, if anyone is in Christ,
the new creation has come:
The old has gone, the new is here!
— 2 Corinthians 5:17

I believe:

God changes lives.

God can redeem any life.

Old things will be passed way and
all things can be made new.

God makes me a better person.

I believe:

My family tree is the Cross of Calvary
and royal blood flows
through my veins.

Mercy can rewrite any story.

Bad beginnings can have happy endings.

God delights in enlarging my influence for Him.

Jabez was more honorable than his brothers.

His mother had named him Jabez, saying,

"I gave birth to him in pain."

Jabez cried out to the God of Israel, "

Oh, that you would bless me and enlarge my

territory! Let your hand be with me, and

keep me from harm so that I will be free from

pain." And God granted his request.

— 1 Chronicles 4:9-10

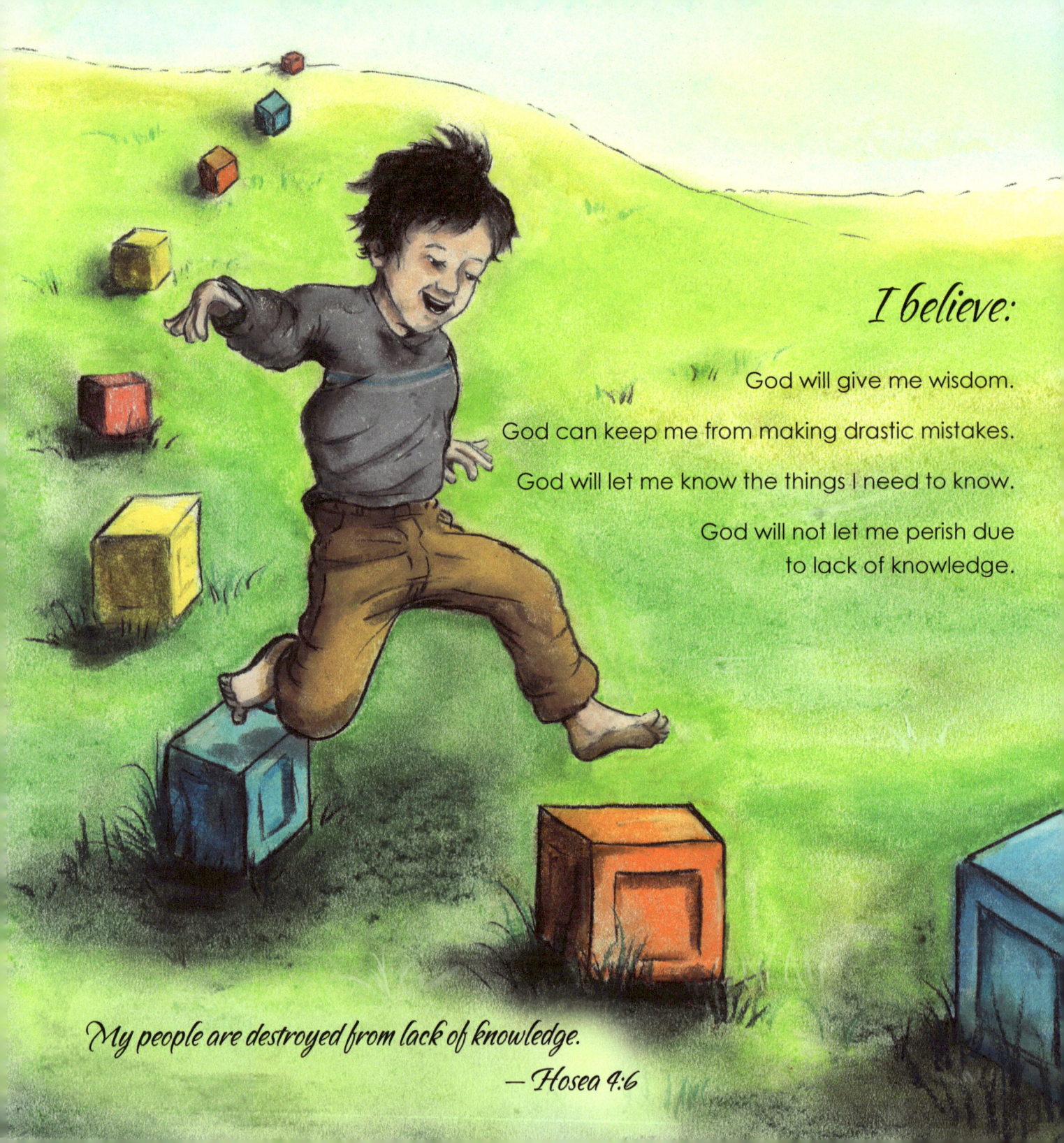

I believe:

God will give me wisdom.

God can keep me from making drastic mistakes.

God will let me know the things I need to know.

God will not let me perish due to lack of knowledge.

My people are destroyed from lack of knowledge.
— Hosea 4:6

I believe:

God will turn my tears into showers of blessing.
I can trade my weakness for God's power through prayer.
God delights in helping me.
God has a perfect plan, purpose, and will for my life.

But he said to me,
"My grace is sufficient for you, for my power
is made perfect in weakness." Therefore I will
boast all the more gladly about my weaknesses,
so that Christ's power may rest on me.

— 2 Corinthians 12:9

I believe:

God has not given me
the spirit of fear.

Perfect love casts
out all fear.

God will perfect that
which concerns me.

God is with me always.

For the Spirit God gave us does not make us timid,

but gives us power, love and self-discipline.

— 2 Timothy 1:7

www.ingramcontent.com/pod-product-compliance
Lightning Source LLC
Chambersburg PA
CBHW041242040426
42445CB00004B/120